History's Greatest Mysteries

HISTORY'S INFAMOUS UNSOLVED CRIMES

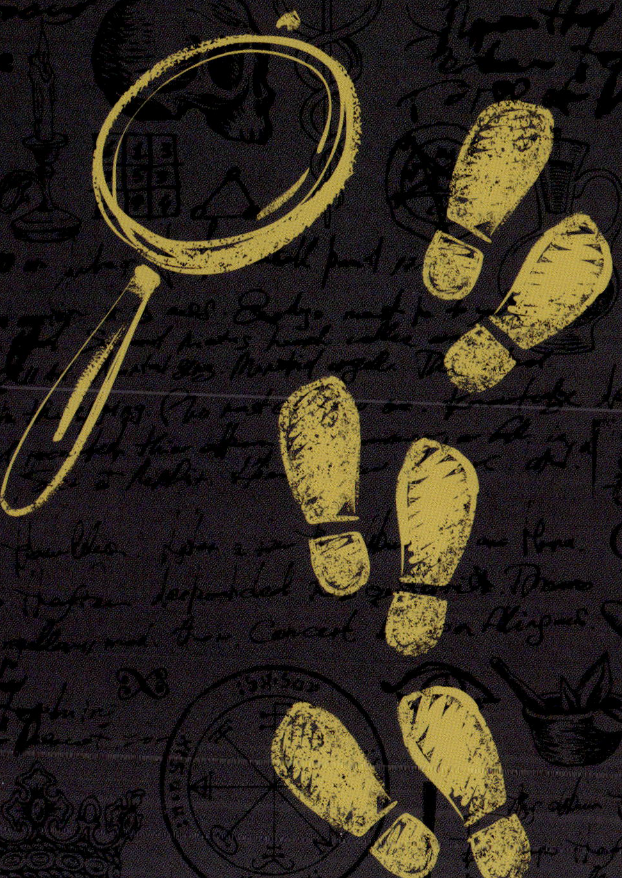

by Grace Hansen

abdobooks.com

Published by Pop!, a division of ABDO, PO Box 398166, Minneapolis, Minnesota 55439. Copyright © 2023 by Abdo Consulting Group, Inc. International copyrights reserved in all countries. No part of this book may be reproduced in any form without written permission from the publisher. DiscoverRoo™ is a trademark and logo of Pop!.

Printed in the United States of America, North Mankato, Minnesota.

052022
092022

THIS BOOK CONTAINS RECYCLED MATERIALS

Cover Photos: Herald Examiner Collection/Los Angeles Public Library

Interior Photos: Shutterstock Images; Getty Images; Herald Examiner Collection/Los Angeles Public Library; UCLA Charles E. Young Research Library Department of Special Collections; National Park Service Archives

Editor: Elizabeth Andrews
Series Designer: Candice Keimig

Library of Congress Control Number: 2021951836
Publisher's Cataloging-in-Publication Data
Names: Hansen, Grace, author.
Title: History's infamous unsolved crimes / by Grace Hansen
Description: Minneapolis, Minnesota : Pop, 2023 | Series: History's greatest mysteries | Includes online resources and index
Identifiers: ISBN 9781098242275 (lib. bdg.) | ISBN 9781644947906 (pbk.) | ISBN 9781098242978 (ebook)
Subjects: LCSH: Cold cases (Criminal investigation)--Juvenile literature. | Unsolved crimes (Cold cases)--Juvenile literature. | Crime--History--Juvenile literature. | Curiosities and wonders--Juvenile literature.
Classification: DDC 364.1--dc23

WELCOME TO DiscoverRoo!

Pop open this book and you'll find QR codes loaded with information, so you can learn even more!

Scan this code* and others like it while you read, or visit the website below to make this book pop!

popbooksonline.com/unsolved-crimes

*Scanning QR codes requires a web-enabled smart device with a QR code reader app and a camera.

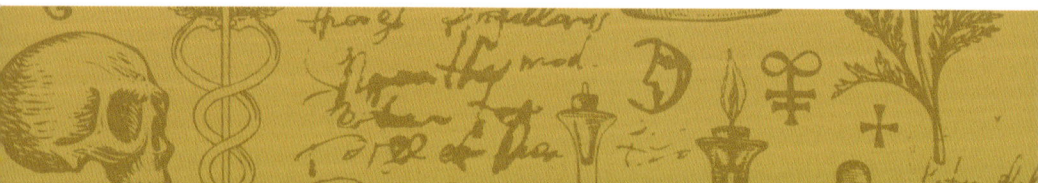

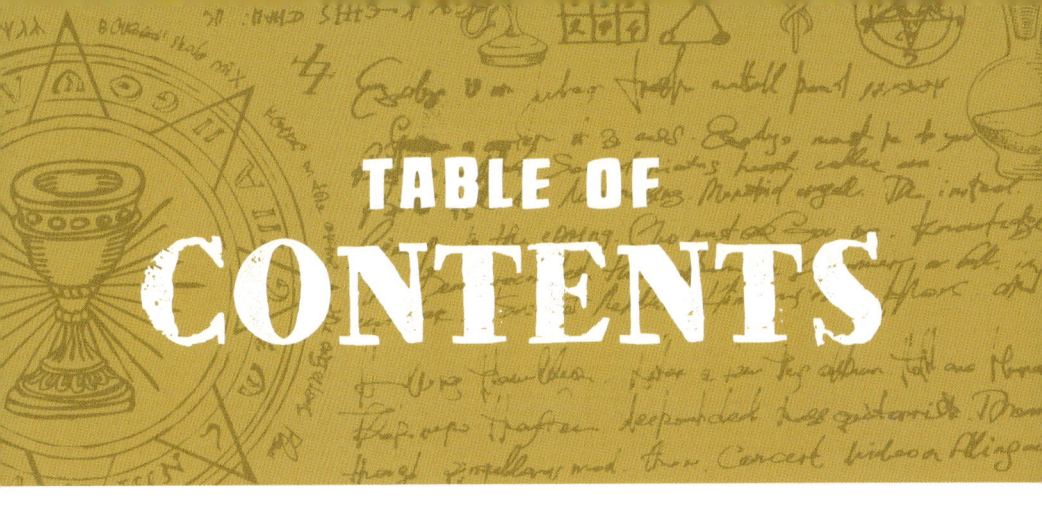

TABLE OF CONTENTS

CHAPTER 1
Unsolved 4

CHAPTER 2
Rembrandt Raid 6

CHAPTER 3
Where's Walter? 14

CHAPTER 4
Escape from Alcatraz 22

Making Connections 30
Glossary 31
Index 32
Online Resources 32

CHAPTER 1

UNSOLVED

Laws have been around to guide people since early times. Those who break the rules are punished accordingly. But what about the criminals who commit the perfect crime? From stolen art to missing

WATCH A VIDEO HERE!

No matter how many leads or clues an investigator has, their case still may never be solved.

people, there are thousands of cases that have not been, and maybe never will be, solved.

CHAPTER 2

REMBRANDT RAID

How does one put a price on three Rembrandt pieces, a rare Vermeer painting, and nine other timeless works of art? Art dealers have tried and decided that the 13 items stolen from the Isabella Stewart Gardner Museum in Boston had a price tag of at least half a billion dollars.

LEARN MORE HERE!

The peaceful courtyard of the Isabella Stewart Gardner Museum

In the early morning hours of March 18, 1990, two young guards on their nightshift walked the museum. Music school dropout Richard E. Abath was one of them. At 12:54, Abath investigated multiple fire alarms, but did not find any smoke or other signs of fire. Exactly 30 minutes later, two policemen buzzed at the door. They claimed to be responding to a call.

The robbers wore fake mustaches to hide their identities.

Abath let them in. The policemen thought they recognized him. "Come here and show us some identification." Before he knew it, Abath was handcuffed. The second guard was also placed under arrest and bound. When he demanded a reason, one of the policemen said, "You're not being arrested. This is a robbery. Don't give us any problems and you won't get hurt."

The guards stayed quiet for what felt like forever while the robbers sliced priceless paintings from their frames. It took 81 minutes for the phony policemen to complete one of the biggest art **heists** in history.

Some of the most valuable stolen works included Rembrandt's A Lady and Gentleman in Black, *a self portrait, and* The Storm on the Sea of Galilee.

The empty frames still hang on the walls in the Isabella Stewart Gardner Museum.

In 2013, the FBI determined that the art had almost certainly been in Connecticut and Philadelphia. But the trails ended after that. To this day, no arrests have been made and no art has been found. The museum still displays the empty frames in remembrance.

DID YOU KNOW? A $10 million dollar reward has been set for information that leads to the recovery of the stolen art.

CHAPTER 3
WHERE'S WALTER?

On a sunny afternoon in Los Angeles, nine-year-old Walter Collins walked down his street with change in his pocket. His mother, Christine, had given it to him to see a movie. The date was March 10, 1928.

COMPLETE AN ACTIVITY HERE!

It was the last day anyone saw Walter alive. At first, police believed he ran away. But Christine insisted her son would never leave her. Neighbors were interviewed. But it led to nothing.

Walter went missing without a trace.

Five months later, Christine received the news she had longed for. Her son had been found in Illinois. She bought her boy's train ticket. When it pulled into the station, Christine's relief turned to panic. She looked to Captain J.J. Jones of the Los Angeles Police Department (LAPD). This boy was not her son. Jones insisted she was confused. "Try the boy out," he told her. Her memory was sure to come back.

Christine never gave up hope that she would one day find Walter.

Christine sued the LAPD. Jones was ordered to pay her $10,800, but never did.

Weeks later, readied with dental records, Christine marched the **impostor** child into the police station. She hoped it was enough proof. Instead, Jones had Christine sent to the hospital. Days passed. Christine was given medicine to help her come to her senses. And then suddenly she was released. The boy, whose real name was Arthur Hutchins Jr, had confessed to pretending to be Walter.

Arthur confessed to faking his identity after being questioned by police, but still gave the fake name Billy Fields.

About 50 miles east of Los Angeles in Riverside, CA, Jessie Clark was visiting her brother Sanford. The boy had been living with his uncle Gordon Northcott and great aunt Sarah Louise Northcott at their chicken ranch. Jessie saw her brother was in a bad situation. She returned home and called the authorities.

Sanford told the police that many boys had died on the farm. The police found remains and items belonging to missing children. Sarah confessed to Walter's death. But there was no sign Walter had ever been there. Gordon denied it but confessed to other crimes. Both were **convicted**.

WHY PRETEND?

Arthur was 12 years old when he impersonated Walter. Arthur said he was told many times that he looked like the missing boy. Because Arthur's life was not great, he decided to start a new one. He also admitted that he wanted to see Hollywood and maybe meet his idol, cowboy Tom Mix.

DID YOU KNOW? Police believed they found Walter's shoes at the Northcott home because its heel was worn similarly to other shoes belonging to the boy. This was the only potential physical evidence linking Walter to the Northcotts.

In October 1930, Christine received a telegram. It was from Gordon. He wanted to see her. When she arrived, he said, "I don't know anything about it [Walter]. I am innocent." Five years later, a different said victim of Gordon turned up alive.

This gave Christine even more hope that Walter was still out there. She held onto this hope until her death in 1964.

Northcott stands before the judge during his murder trial in Riverside, California.

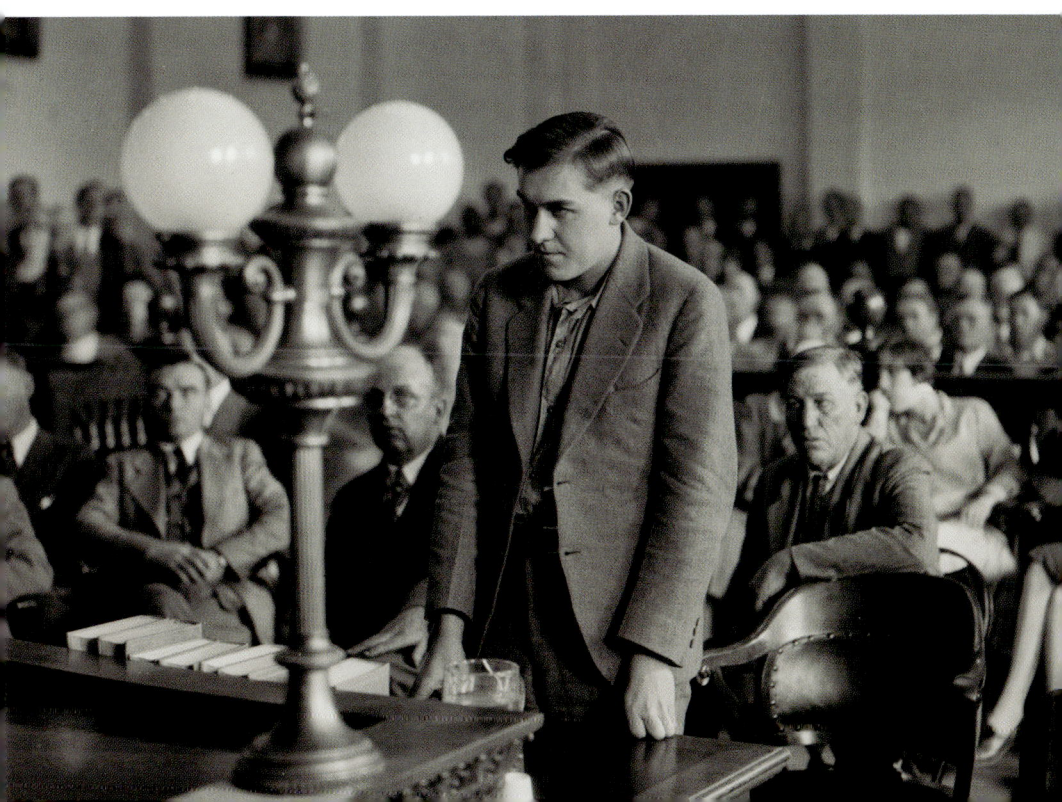

CHAPTER 4
ESCAPE FROM ALCATRAZ

Alcatraz Island sits in the middle of San Francisco Bay. The island began taking prisoners during the Civil War. In 1934, a maximum-security prison was built on it. The prison had guard towers, iron bars, harsh rules, and at least one guard for every three prisoners. But what better

EXPLORE LINKS HERE!

security is there than being surrounded by cold, rough, shark-infested water?

Over the years, plots and attempts by prisoners to escape were numerous. Just three men ever manged to break free. And it wasn't simple.

Alcatraz Island is one of 18 islands in San Francisco Bay. Angel Island is about 2.5 miles (4km) north of Alcatraz Island.

June 12, 1962, began like any day at Alcatraz. Guards walked down Cell Block B to complete morning bed checks. A guard came to Frank Morris's cell. Morris was still asleep. The guard reached through the bars to shake Morris awake. A plaster-like head with human hair rolled off the pillow and onto the floor. He yelled to the others. The guards quickly realized brothers John and Clarence Anglin were missing too. Alcatraz went into lockdown!

A utility corridor was just behind the men's cells.

The men planned to ride their raft more than two miles to Angel Island and then to the mainland. Within two days of the escape, letters belonging to the men washed ashore. A homemade life vest and paddles were also recovered. No one knows if the prisoners ever made it to shore.

MAKING CONNECTIONS

TEXT-TO-SELF

If you were an investigator looking into an unsolved crime, what kinds of things would you do to help solve the case?

TEXT-TO-TEXT

Have you read any other books about unsolved crimes? Why were the crimes in those books so difficult to solve?

TEXT-TO-WORLD

Do you think it's important for investigators to look into old, unsolved crimes? Why or why not?

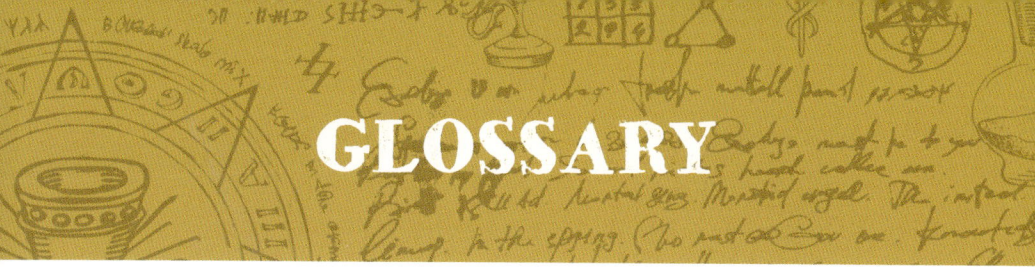

GLOSSARY

convicted – found guilty of a crime.

heist – a planned robbery, especially one in which art, jewelry or a large sum of money is taken.

impersonate – to copy the appearance and actions of; pretend to be.

impostor – a person who tricks or cheats others by pretending to be another person.

utility corridor – a hallway through which electrical, water supply, and sewer lines pass.

ventilator – something that ventilates, especially a device that pulls out foul air and draws in clean, fresh air.

INDEX

Alcatraz Island, 22
Alcatraz prison, 22—28
Angel Island, 29
Anglin, Clarence, 24—29
Anglin, John, 24—29
Boston, MA, 6
Collins, Christine, 14—21
Collins, Walter, 14—17, 19—21
FBI, 13, 26
Hutchins Jr., Arthur, 17—19
Isabella Stewart Gardner Museum, 6—13
LAPD, 16—17
Morris, Frank, 24—29
Northcott, Gordon, 18—20
Northcott, Sarah L., 18—19
San Francisco, CA, 22, 29
West, Allen, 26—27

ONLINE RESOURCES
popbooksonline.com

Scan this code* and others like it while you read, or visit the website below to make this book pop!

popbooksonline.com/unsolved-crimes

*Scanning QR codes requires a web-enabled smart device with a QR code reader app and a camera.